LOOM
Magic Xtreme!

25 Spectacular, Never-Before-Seen
Designs for Rainbows of Fun

John McCann,
Becky Thomas &
Monica Sweeney

Sky Pony Press
New York

Sky Pony Press books may be purchased in bulk at special discounts for sales promotion, corporate gifts, fund-raising, or educational purposes. Special editions can also be created to specifications. For details, contact the Special Sales Department, Sky Pony Press, 307 West 36th Street, 11th Floor, New York, NY 10018 or info@skyhorsepublishing.com.

Sky Pony® is a registered trademark of Skyhorse Publishing, Inc.®, a Delaware corporation.

Visit our website at www.skyponypress.com.

10 9 8 7 6 5 4 3 2 1

Manufactured in the United States of America, December 2013
This product conforms to CPSIA 2008 .

Library of Congress Cataloguing-in-Publication Data is available on file.

ISBN: 978-1-62914-342-2

CONTENTS

ACKNOWLEDGMENTS

We would like to thank our great editor, Kelsie Besaw, for her continued support on all of our endeavors. Thank you to Bill Wolfsthal, Tony Lyons, and Linda Biagi for making this project possible. A big thank you to everyone at Skyhorse who continue to do a wonderful job with this series. And our Xtreme thanks go to Allan Penn and Holly Schmidt for their creative collaboration and guidance throughout this project.

Thank you to all of the smiling faces of *Loom Magic Xtreme!*: Lucy Bartlett, Katelyn Clarke, Quisi Cohen, Morgan Glovsky, Alex Johnson, Jax and Nick Kordes, Charlotte and Griffin Penn, Raya Smith, and Ella Stanwood.

Special thanks to Nick Kordes for contributing the original design for the Glow-in-the-Dark Skeleton Hand.

GLOSSARY

hook: The hook is the off-white, hook-shaped utensil provided in the packaging of your loom. This is used to remove rubber bands from their pegs.

mini-loom: Provided with the original packaging in your loom, this is a blue plastic tube that looks like a capital T. This loom is a handy way to make chains like the fishtail stitch without using a large loom. To make this stitch, bands stacked on the mini-loom are moved with your hook and placed in the center gap over and over. Pull the chain out from the slit in the side so it doesn't stay inside the tube.

c-clip: A c-clip, as its name suggests, is a small, clear clip shaped like a "c" that we use to hold rubber bands together and are often the last step in a project. Some rubber band kits come with s-clips instead.

cap band: The cap band acts like a stopper for the last band on the loom, which prevents other bands from coming off the peg.

double-loop: When you need to use a cap band, "double-loop" means that you will wrap the rubber band (or bands) twice on a peg.

triple-loop: Just like the double-looped cap band, but with one more twist!

Set up your loom square: When all of the columns are evenly set on the loom; no column of pegs is set forward or backward.

offset: When columns in the loom are not square. For example, when the outside columns are set evenly and the middle column is set one peg closer to you.

"Looping" your project back: This is the last step before you remove your project from the loom. It connects your bands to each other instead of just to the loom.

To Loop Your Project:

1. Start at the peg indicated in the instructions: usually it is the last or second-to-last peg in your project, or the peg where you have put a cap band.

2. Use your plastic hook tool and slide it into the hollow space in the middle of the peg to grab the top un-looped band on the peg.

3. Then pull the band up and off the peg, pulling it through any cap bands or any looped bands stacked above it.

4. Attach the band on your hook to the peg where the other end of the same band is still attached. If there is more than one band, loop all of the bands on a peg before you move on to loop the next peg.

5. Pegs are typically looped in the opposite order from how you laid them out on the loom, but pay attention to any specific instructions for a project.

6. When you have finished looping your project, you should have a few loose loops remaining on the last peg on the loom: you need to secure those loops by tying a band around them or using a c-clip, or your project will unravel!

HEART EARRINGS

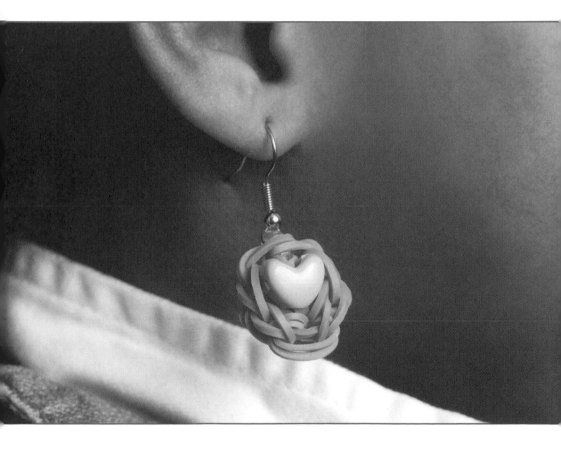

Cupid could not have done it better himself! Incredibly simple and lots of fun, these heart earrings are great to give to your friends as gifts or to accessorize your outfit. These adorable heart earrings are super stylish for the fashionista in you!

Difficulty level: **Easy**

You need:

1 loom • hook • 2 c-clips • 2 heart beads • 2 "fish hook" style earrings • 18 rubber bands

1. Set up your loom with the pegs square and the arrow pointing away from you.

2. Lay out a small pentagon shape onto your loom: lay a line of two bands across the bottom row, moving left to right. Attach a band from each corner peg in the first row, and connect it to the next peg above it. Attach a band to each of the outside pegs in the second row, and connect them to the middle peg in the third row.

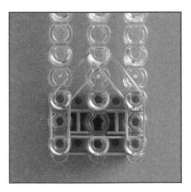

3. Attach a band to the second middle peg, and connect it to the peg to the right. Thread a band through a heart bead, attach one end of the band to the first middle peg, and connect it to the middle peg above it.

4. Attach a band to the middle peg in the second row, and connect it to the peg to the left. Attach another band to the second middle peg, and connect it to the peg above it.

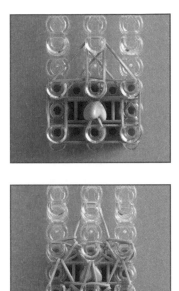

5. Triple-loop a cap band, and put it on the middle peg in the second row.

6. Starting at the middle peg in the second row, hook the band below the triple-looped band, and pull it off the peg, looping it back onto the peg where it began. Once you have finished looping the center peg, loop the top center peg, then the two outside pegs in the second row, then the two outside pegs in the first row.

7. Secure the loose bands on the final peg with a c-clip. Carefully pull the bands off of the loom.

8. To attach an earring hook to the top of the heart pendant, pull one of the top bands in the shape or the plastic c-clip through the metal loop of the earring hook.

9. Repeat this process for the second pendant.

10. Pair with a fun matching outfit!

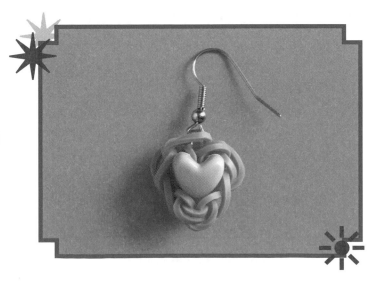

GLOW-iN-THE-DARK
SKELETON HAND

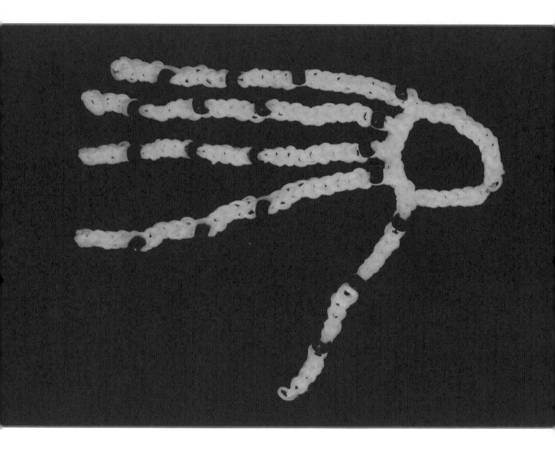

Show your handiwork with this awesome glow-in-the-dark project! This rubber band hand wraps around your wrist and fingers to imitate a creepy skeleton hand, and the best part is what happens when you turn out the lights! If you are making this project for a smaller hand, reduce the number of bands you loop onto pegs for steps 4, 6, 8, and 9 for the fingers, and 17, 19, and 21 for the thumb. Anything that glows in the dark usually needs to soak up some light first, so just make sure to keep the project in lots of light before you want it to glow in the dark.

Difficulty level: **Medium**

You need:

1 loom • hook • 5 c-clips • 19 black beads • 290 glow-in-the-dark rubber bands

1. To begin this project, set up your loom by connecting two columns to make one long column on the loom.

2. Attach two rubber bands over the first peg and onto the second peg along the column.

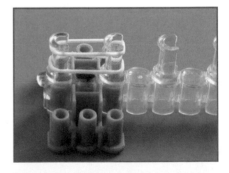

3. Thread two rubber bands together through a black bead. Attach one side of the beaded bands to the second peg and the other side to the third peg.

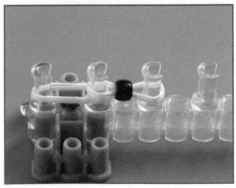

4. Attach two bands over the third and fourth pegs, this time without beads. Repeat this process until you reach the eleventh peg in the column. (For smaller hands, you may stop attaching loops at an earlier peg.)

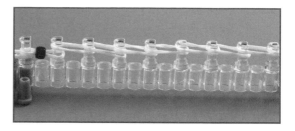

5. Thread two bands through another black bead, and place the bands around the next pegs (the eleventh and twelfth pegs).

6. Continue to lay out your line of double bands for the next four pegs.

7. Thread two bands through a bead, and attach it from the most recent peg to the one after it.

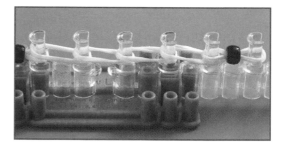

8. Lay out your line of double bands for the next four pegs, then bead the next two bands before placing them on the next pegs on the loom.

9. Continue to lay out your line of double bands to the end of the loom.

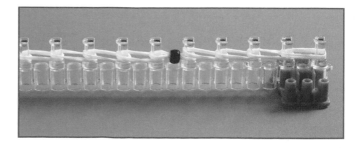

10. Double-loop a cap band over the last peg.

11. Turn your loom around so that the arrow is facing you. Starting with the peg where you placed your cap band, begin looping your bands back to the peg where they started. Continue looping all of the bands until you make your way to the other end of the loom where you started laying out your bands.

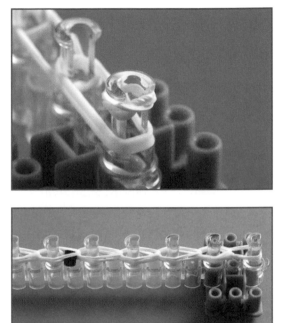

12. Once you have reached the end of the loom, attach a c-clip. This c-clip is just to keep the project together while you continue working, but will eventually be removed when you connect all of the fingers to the hand.

13. Remove the project from the loom and set aside.

14. Repeat steps 1 through 13 three times to make the remaining fingers.

15. To make the thumb, you will be repeating a similar process as the fingers, but with fewer bands and just three black beads.

16. Attach two rubber bands to the first and second peg.

17. Thread two bands through a black bead, and attach it from the second peg to the third.

18. Lay out a line of double bands for the next five pegs. Bead the next pair of bands before placing it on the loom. Lay out non-beaded double bands for another four pegs. Thread the next pair of bands through a bead before placing them on the loom. Lay out a line of non-beaded double bands for the next four pegs.

19. Double-loop a cap band over the last peg.

20. Turn your loom around so that the arrow is facing you. Using your hook, loop the band beneath the cap band to the peg where it came from. Loop all the bands in this way until you reach the end of the loom.

21. Attach a c-clip to the final loose loops on the loom, then remove your thumb and set it aside.

22. To make the "wrist," or bracelet portion, lay out a line of double bands all the way down your double-length loom (or less for smaller wrists).

23. Double-loop a cap band over the last peg.

24. To put the skeleton hand together, you will need to connect the ends of the "fingers" to different pegs spread out on the loom. Begin with the "thumb," and wrap the beaded end of it (where you had held it together with a c-clip) over the third peg from the cap band.

25. After the thumb, connect the "fingers" to every other peg.

26. Starting from the peg with the cap band, loop each of the bands back to their original pegs until you reach the end of the loom.

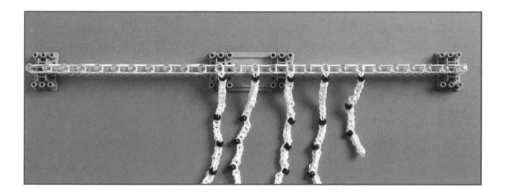

27. Connect a c-clip to the last rubber band, and remove everything from the loom.

28. Complete the wrist by connecting the ends together, either by tying with an extra band or by connecting the end with the c-clip to the opposite end.

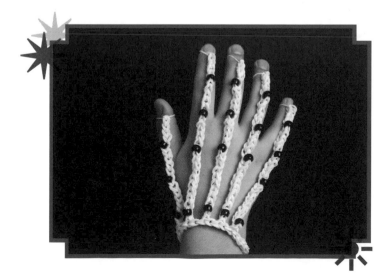

POOF BALL BRACELET

This three-dimensional bracelet is a bouncy masterpiece: all it takes is a single chain and a handful of poof balls. Follow our example to make the poof balls two-toned, or you can make them all one color. Use all the colors you have to make a crazy multicolored bracelet!

Difficulty level: **Easy**

You need:

1 loom • 4–5 c-clips • scissors • 112 rubber bands

1. Loop eight bands together as shown to make a chain, alternating your colors.

2. Set up your loom with the middle pegs removed. Stretch your chain onto the loom like in the picture, so that it crisscrosses the center of the loom.

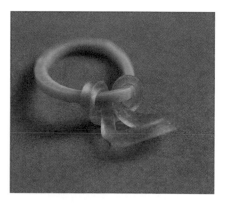

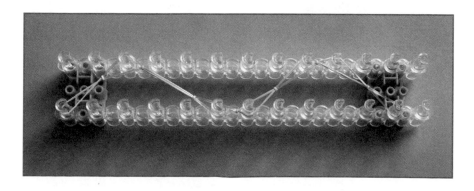

3. Take two bands and connect them together as shown. Connect all but eight of the remaining bands in the same way (you should knot ninety-six bands, enough to make forty-eight total knotted bands).

4. Stretch one of your tied rubber bands onto the loom at an angle. Take another tied band and stretch it onto the loom at the opposite angle, so that the knots overlap and make an X shape. The knot should also

overlap the chain of bands that will make up the base of your bracelet. Stack a total of twelve knotted bands in this way. Repeat three more times, working your way down the loom to make four total poof balls on your bracelet.

5. Take a band and loop it around the middle of your X shape. Secure the band with a c-clip. Do the same for the three other X shapes.

6. Take another band and loop it around the middle of your X shape in the other direction. Secure that band with the same c-clip you used to

secure the last band. Do the same for the rest of the X shapes on the loom.

7. Carefully pull the bracelet off the loom. Be careful not to pull any of the loops out of your poof balls as you remove them.

8. Use your scissors to cut through the loops of your poof balls. Don't cut the bands holding the poof balls together!

TWiSTY HEADBAND

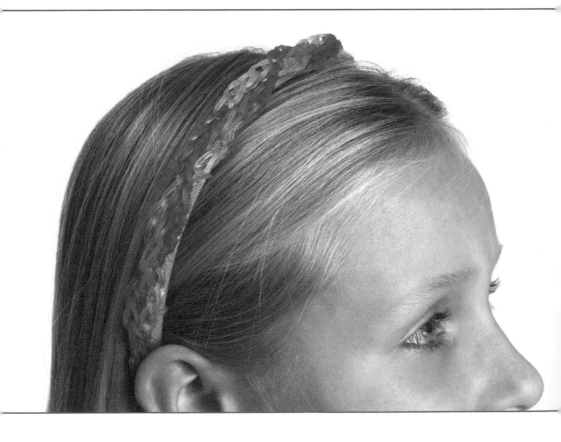

Don't just accessorize with bracelets and necklaces–make headbands, too! This cute jewelry accent is so pretty it can be worn with just about anything. Using a simple braid-like stitch, you can make a plain-looking headband into something really special!

Difficulty level: **Easy**

You need:

1 loom • 1 mini-loom • hook • 2 c-clips • 1 plain headband • 50 rubber bands (colors shown: teal, purple, and pink)

1. Set up your loom with the middle pegs closer to you and the arrow pointing away. Starting on the middle peg closest to you, lay out an oval shape. Lay out the right side of the oval first, then lay out the left side in the same way.

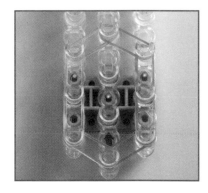

2. Repeat this pattern all the way down the loom, laying out four oval shapes. Start each new oval shape on the middle peg where you ended your last one, and lay out the right side before you do the left.

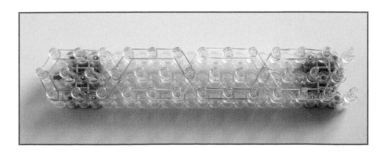

3. Triple-loop a cap band around the peg where you end your last oval shape.

4. Starting at the cap band peg, hook the first band beneath the triple-loop and pull it up and off the peg, looping it back onto the peg where it started. Always loop the top band on the peg first, then the next one down, until you have looped all the bands on the peg. Continue looping the rest of the bands in this way, making your way to the other end of the loom.

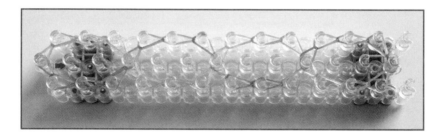

5. When you have looped all the bands on your loom, you will have two bands left on the last peg; slide these bands onto your plastic hook to secure them, then remove the rest of the project from the loom.

6. Lay out your four oval patterns again, as you did in step 2. Instead of placing a cap band over the last peg as you did before, slide the loops of the finished stitch off the plastic hook and onto the peg.

7. Loop your pattern as you did in step 4, starting at the peg where you attached the finished stitch. Secure the loose loops with the plastic hook again and pull the finished stitch off the loom.

8. Lay out your pattern one more time, and stack the loose end of the finished stitch on the final peg. Loop your project as you did before. Secure the final loose bands with a c-clip.

9. Using your loom or mini-loom, make a single chain of bands long enough to fit over your headband without stretching.

10. Hook the end of your chain to the end of your other stitch by securing it to the same c-clip. Hold the c-clip at the end of the headband, and loop a band around the headband and your rubber band braid, just above the clip.

11. From the other side of the headband, slide several double-looped bands onto the headband, spaced about an inch apart.

12. Thread the single chain through the first loop of the other stitch, then thread it through one of the double-looped bands on the headband. Bring the single chain back up through the next loop of the stitch. Adjust the project so that the place

where the single chain is secured to the headband is covered by the other stitch.

13. Continue to secure the rubber bands to the headband in this way, weaving the single chain through the other stitch and tucking it under the double-looped bands. When you reach the other end of the headband, loop a rubber band tightly just above the c-clip, as you did for the other side.

MiNi-LOOM
NAMe BRACeLeT

Make a name for yourself by testing your mini-loom skills with this awesome bracelet! Whether you use letters to tag your own name, a friend's, or your favorite sports team, this great bracelet is sure to wow!

Difficulty level: **Easy**

You need:

1 mini-loom • hook • c-clip • 2 decorative beads • letter beads • enough bands for a bracelet

1. Attach a rubber band to the mini-loom in a figure 8.

2. Attach another rubber band over the first, but do not twist it.

3. Stack a third rubber band above the other two, without twisting it.

4. Unhook the bottom rubber band on the loom, using your hook to pull it off the loom. Drop the loops in the middle of the loom.

5. Stack another rubber band on top of the two bands remaining on the loom.

6. Hook the bottom band off the loom and into the gap as you did before. Repeat this step, pulling the "tail" of the completed loops to the side of the loom with the slit down the side. Continue until you have a few inches of bracelet completed.

7. Thread the next band through a bead before putting it on the mini-loom as usual.

8. Hook the bottom band off the mini-loom and into the gap: hold your bead in place with your fingers if you need to until you finish the stitch and the band is secure. Complete three more non-beaded bands.

9. Thread the next band through the first letter bead in the name or word you are spelling. Turn the bead so that the bottom of the letter is facing away from your project "tail."

10. With your beaded band in place, continue looping as you did before. Stack another non-beaded band on top of the loom and complete a regular stitch. Repeat this twice more to complete three non-beaded stitches on top of your bead.

11. Thread a band through the next letter bead and loop it onto the mini-loom. Complete three more non-beaded stitches. Repeat until you have finished your word or name.

12. Complete three more non-beaded bands, then bead a band and complete the stitch.

13. Continue to stack rubber bands on top of the loop and unloop them from the bottom until you have made a chain long enough for a bracelet.

14. Run your hook through the two bands on the loom and pull them off.

15. Attach a c-clip to the last two bands to finish your bracelet.

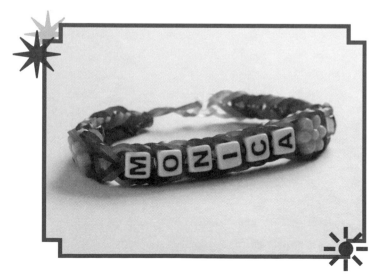

COVERED
HOOP EARRINGS

Jazz up your jewelry with these stylish hoop earrings! Not only are these earrings super cute and fun, but they are also incredibly simple to make! A loom is not required for this project, so you can add a little flair to your earrings wherever you are. This project uses large hoop earrings that you can find in most craft stores and inexpensive jewelry shops. If you prefer to try this project on smaller hoops, just make sure the hoops are sturdy and the latch will allow you to slide a bead over it. Hoops that are too thin make it harder to knot your bands and will create a very loose stitch. Now pick your favorite colors, some funky beads, and make this new addition to your jewelry box!

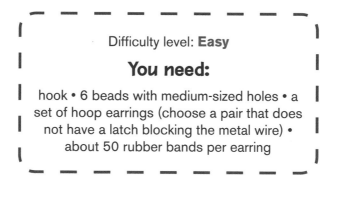

Difficulty level: **Easy**

You need:

hook • 6 beads with medium-sized holes • a set of hoop earrings (choose a pair that does not have a latch blocking the metal wire) • about 50 rubber bands per earring

1. Using just the rubber bands and your fingers, loop one rubber band through another and knot it on itself. This will hold the beginning of your stitch in place.

2. Moving on to the free rubber band, squish the band in half with your fingers so that it forms a half-moon shape.

3. Insert your next rubber band through the loops of the first band.

4. Squish this band to form another half-moon. Insert another rubber band to repeat the process.

5. Repeat this process until you have a long chain of interlocking rubber bands. Alternate the colors in a color pattern that you really like, or follow the model and switch between pink, green, and blue repeatedly.

6. For large hoops like the ones in the photographs, the chain should be much longer than the circumference of the hoop, about forty to fifty bands long.

7. Knot the other end of the stitch so that the chain does not fall apart.

8. Slide the first band at the end of the chain around the post side of the hoop (not the backing).

9. With the first band around the hoop earring, twist the next band and slide it onto the hoop. Slide it through the same loop in the band where the next band in the chain is connected. This will keep your loops neat.

10. With the next band in the chain, repeat by twisting the band and sliding it over the hoop.

11. Repeat this about eight times, and then slide your bead over the metal earring. You do not need to slide the bead over the rubber bands.

12. Continue to loop the bands about eight times, and add your second bead.

13. If you are running out of room on the earring, just slide the bands toward the back of the hoop so they are closely packed.

14. Continue to loop the bands another eight times, and slide the last bead over the earring.

15. Loop the remaining bands, continuing to slide the chain along the hoop so the bands are closely packed.

16. Knot the last band and snip off any loose ends with scissors, being careful not to cut the other bands.

17. If you find the bands are popping off the end of the earring, it is because the chain is too long. Simply cut out a couple of the bands at the end and knot the last one.

18. Repeat this process for the second hoop earring.

PiRATe EYePATCH

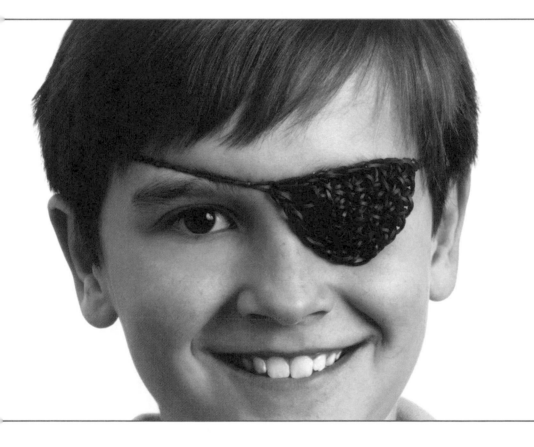

Say *ARRR!* for this awesome pirate eye patch! Whether you are heading out on the high seas or finding buried treasure in your backyard, your own pirate eye patch will have you giving Captain Hook a run for his money! Great for Halloween, a play, or for some after-school fun, you and your maties can look like the baddest pirates in town!

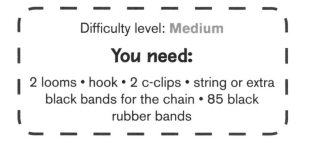

Difficulty level: **Medium**

You need:

2 looms • hook • 2 c-clips • string or extra black bands for the chain • 85 black rubber bands

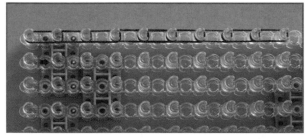

1. Set up two looms, side by side, with the pegs square and the arrow pointing away from you.

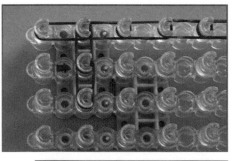

2. In the far left column, start at the peg closest to you and lay out a line of nine black bands.

3. Start at the second peg in the far left column and loop two bands to the right.

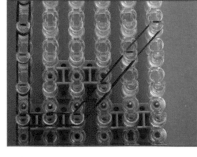

4. Starting at the peg where you ended your last band, lay out three bands moving up and to the right.

5. Lay out the rest of the eye patch outline: from the peg where you ended your last diagonal band, lay out a line of two bands in the far right column, then lay out three diagonal bands, moving up and to the left. From the last peg of your

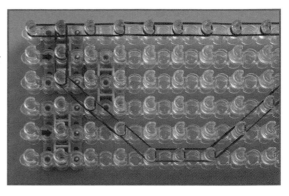

diagonal bands, lay out a line of two bands to finish your eye patch outline.

6. Start filling in your eye patch shape with bands. Attach a band each around the second and third pegs in the second row, and connect them to the next peg above. Starting on the third peg in the far left column, lay out a line of three bands going across from left to right.

7. Repeat this pattern for the rest of the eye patch shape, first laying out vertical bands on all the inside pegs to connect them to the next row above, then laying out horizontal lines starting at the far left and moving from left to right until you reach the edge of the eye patch shape on the right.

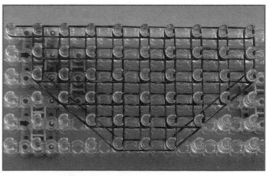

8. Attach a band around the tenth peg in the far left column, and connect it to the peg above.

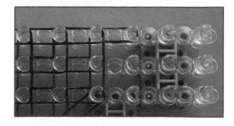

9. Loop your bands back to the pegs where they started, beginning on the tenth peg in the far left column. Hook the band just below the top band (the last one you laid down) and pull it up and off the peg, looping it back to the peg where it started. Loop the rest of the bands on the peg this way, working from top to bottom. Loop the rest of the pegs in the pattern in the same way, working your way to the end of the loom where you began laying out your shape. Secure the final loops with a c-clip.

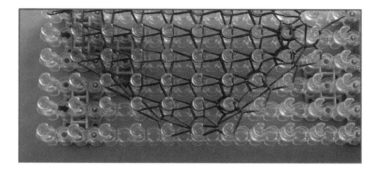

10. Use string or loop two chains of black bands to create the band for your eye patch. Tie one of the chains around the loops you secured with the c-clip and remove the c-clip. Tie the other end to the loop at the other end of the eye patch. You can connect these two chains with a c-clip.

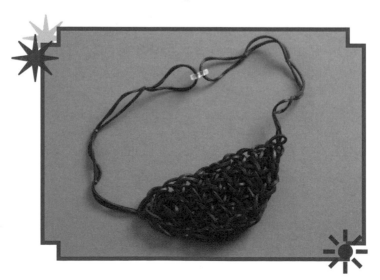

BOUQUET OF FLOWERS

Who knew rubber bands could be so pretty?! These adorable rubber band flowers make a really nice gift for family and friends, or they can be used to decorate your room! The best part is, you will never have to water them! These instructions explain how to make one flower. For a whole bouquet, just repeat the steps using your favorite colors.

Difficulty level: Medium

You need:

1 loom • hook • c-clip • 1 bendable craft wire (about 12 inches in length, or slightly longer than the loom) • 25 white rubber bands • 30 yellow bands • 15 red rubber bands • 26 green rubber bands

To Make the Flower:

1. Set up two looms side by side with the pegs square and the arrows facing away from you.

2. Attach a band around the two middle pegs in the second row.

3. Lay out a circle-like shape onto your loom: start on the left peg of the pegs where you just looped your band, and lay out two diagonal bands going outward, then one up, then two diagonal bands going inward to end your shape.

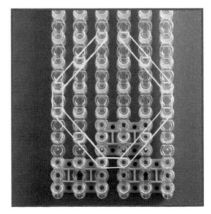

4. Do the same for the right side of the circle, starting at the middle peg on the right.

5. Attach a band around each of the two middle pegs in the second row where you laid your first band, and connect them to the next peg above.

6. Attach a band around the two middle pegs in the third row.

7. Lay out another circle shape inside the shape you just created, putting your bands on the loom the same way you did before: start with the third middle peg on the left, and attach a band diagonally out, then one up, then one diagonally in.

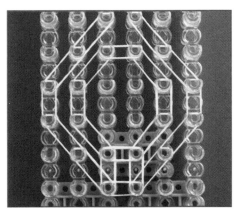

8. Lay out the right side the same way. Attach a band around the top two pegs in your small circle to finish the shape.

9. Starting at the second peg from the left in the third row, lay out a line of three bands, moving from left to right.

10. Repeat step 9, starting on the second peg from the left in the sixth row.

11. Connect the inner and outer circle shapes on both sides: attach a band around the fourth peg in the far left column, and connect it to the peg to the right.

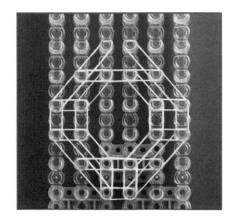

12. Do the same with the fifth peg in the left column. Repeat on the far right side.

13. Attach a band around each of the top two pegs of your shape, and connect them to the peg below.

14. Fill in the center of your circle/flower shape with bands of a different color. Start with the two middle pegs in the third row, and 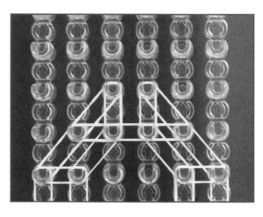 connect them to the pegs above them.

15. Move to the fourth row and lay out a line of three bands, starting on the second peg from the left.

16. Connect the two middle pegs in the fourth row to the pegs above them.

17. Move up to the fifth row and lay out a line of three bands, as you did in the fourth row. Connect the two middle pegs in the fifth row to the pegs above them.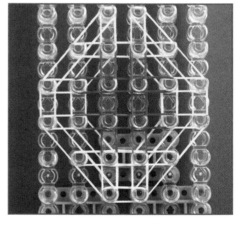

18. Double-loop a cap band around the two middle bands in the seventh row, at the top of your circle shape.

19. Lay out your "petal" bands around the outside of the big circle shape. Start on

the bottom left and continue moving clockwise around the big circle shape, attaching two bands to each peg around the circle until you reach the top of the circle.

20. Then do the same on the right side of the circle. For the pegs on the far right and far left columns, where there is only one free peg to attach your petal bands, leave the other petal band loose on the peg, as shown.

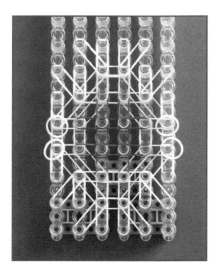

21. Start on the left of the two pegs you double-looped in step 10 and begin looping your rubber bans up and off the peg and hooking them back onto the peg where it started.

22. Loop each peg in your circle shape (the yellow and red bands in our example), moving from left to right in each row, then starting again on the next row down and moving left to right.

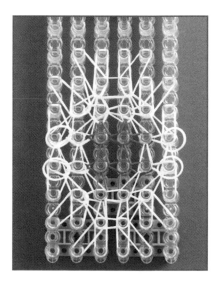

23. Finish looping at the bottom right, and secure the loose band with a c-clip.

To Make the Stem:

1. Set up your loom with the middle column set one peg closer to you and the arrow pointing away from you.

2. Attach a green band to the first middle peg, and connect it to the next peg up and to the left.

3. Connect that peg to the next peg up and to the right.

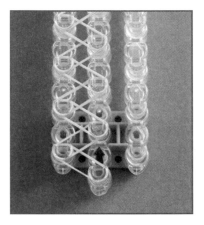

4. Continue to lay out this zigzag pattern all the way up the loom.

5. Cut a length of craft wire a half inch longer than you want your stem to be (ask an adult for help when cutting wire).

6. Lay your wire on top of the zigzag pattern you made on your loom.

7. Turn your loom around so the arrow is pointing toward you. Starting with the middle peg in the row now closest to you, loop the bottom band on each peg over the craft wire and back to the peg where it started.

8. Continue looping the zigzag pattern back toward the beginning of the pattern where you started.

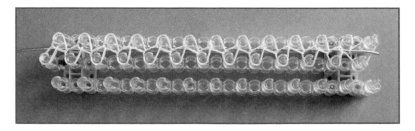

9. Secure the loose loops on the last middle peg on your plastic hook and pull all the bands off the loom.

10. Lay the zigzag pattern out on the loom again, and slide the loose loops from the plastic hook on top of the last peg on the loom.

11. Loop the bands over the craft wire as you did before.

12. Repeat until you cover your whole stem.

13. To attach your stem to the flower, push the wire through the middle of the flower. Bend the end over, as you did with the other end of the stem, to attach it to the loops in the middle of the flower.

14. Repeat this project for as many flowers as you would like in your bouquet!

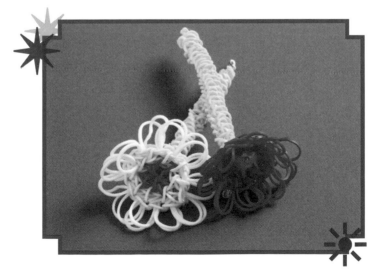

OCTOPUS

Like nothing you have ever seen, this amazing octopus blows other rubber band projects out of the water! This purple sea creature and his creepy, crawly tentacles are actually super simple to put together! Gather lots of rubber bands in colors fit for a deep sea–diving cephalopod and get working on this crazy creation. (Warning: we cannot guarantee this octopus will actually swim!)

Difficulty level: **Easy**

You need:

1 loom • 1 mini-loom • hook • 9 c-clips • 2 googly eyes • about 400 rubber bands (colors shown: pink, purple, and metallic purple)

1. Loop a band in a figure eight on the mini-loom.

2. Loop two more bands on top of the first. Do not twist them. Alternate your colors as you go.

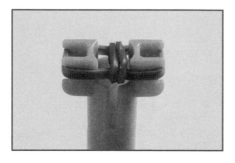

3. Use your plastic hook to pull the bottom band on the mini-loom up and over the other two, and drop the loop in the middle gap of the mini-loom.

4. Stack another band on top of the mini-loom. Hook the bottom band, pull it over the other two, and drop the loop in the middle gap of the mini-loom.

5. Continue adding and looping bands this way to make a chain. When your chain gets long enough after a few bands, pull it through the side of the mini-loom with the slit so that it does not go down the tube of the mini-loom.

6. When your chain is about six inches long, hook the two last loops off the loom and secure them with a c-clip. Loop the other end through a single band and secure it with a c-clip.

7. Make another chain on the mini-loom the same length as the first. Remove it from the loom and secure it with a c-clip. Then slide it onto the single band with the first.

8. Repeat until you have made eight chains, sliding each onto the single band.

9. Loop a band around the bundle of chains, and slide it to the middle.

10. Add some glue and googly eyes to finish the face!

BACON AND EGGS
BREAKFAST

Make a delicious breakfast of champions with your
looms! While we do not recommend eating these
delicious-looking bacon and eggs, this breakfast-themed
project is a cool way to mix things up! This project
requires multiple looms, so it is a great craft to enjoy with
a bunch of your friends. Bon appétit!

Difficulty level:
Bacon: **Easy**   Eggs: **Hard**

You need:

BACON: 1 loom • c-clip • about 50 rubber
bands (colors shown: brown and white)
EGGS: 3 looms • 2 c-clips • about 100 rubber
bands (colors shown: white and yellow)

To Make the Bacon:

1. Set up your loom square with the arrow pointing away from
   you. Lay out a single chain of white bands down the middle
   column, all the way to the end of the loom.

2. Lay out two brown
   bands across the
   first row of the
   loom, moving from
   left to right.

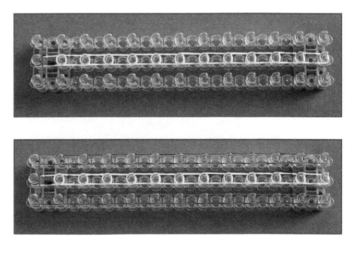

3. Lay out a single
   chain of brown
   bands down the
   right and left
   columns, all the
   way to the end of
   the loom.

4. Lay out two brown bands across each row of the loom as you did in step 2, moving from left to right all the way down the loom.

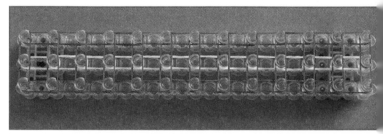

5. Triple-loop a white cap band onto the middle peg in the last row on the loom.

6. Starting on the same peg, hook the band just below the cap-band. Pull the band up and off the peg and loop it back onto the peg where it started. Do the same with the other bands on the peg, working your way down. When you have finished the middle peg, loop the two outer pegs in the row in the same way. Then move to the next row and repeat this step until all the pegs have been looped.

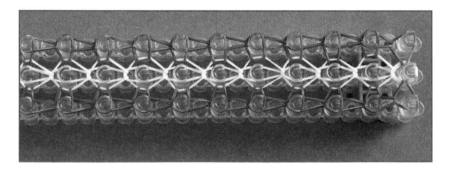

7. Repeat steps 1 to 6 to make more bacon.

To Make the Eggs:

1. Set up three looms side by side. The two outside looms should be offset with the middle pegs pulled toward you, and the middle loom should be offset with the outside columns pulled toward you.

2. Lay out a sunny-side-up egg shape onto the loom.

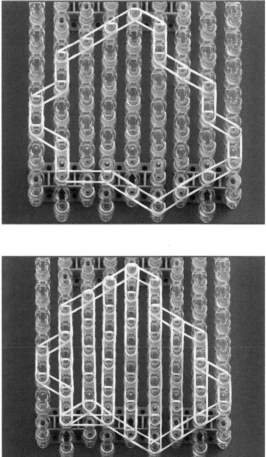

3. Fill the inside of your egg shape: start on the fifth peg up in the second column from the left, and connect it to the peg below it. Connect that peg to the peg below it. Move to the next column, at the top edge of the egg shape, and lay out another single chain down that column until you reach the bottom edge of the egg shape. Continue filling the egg shape this way, changing to yellow bands for the yolk.

4. Fill in your egg shape diagonally: start on the fifth peg up in the second column, and connect it to the next peg up and to the right. Continue laying out bands in this line, moving from left to right until you reach the edge of the egg shape.

Move down to the next diagonal row, and lay out a single chain in the same way. Change to yellow bands when you lay out the bands for the yolk.

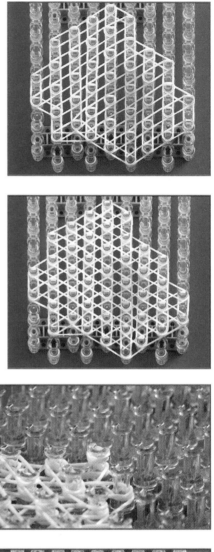

5. Fill in your egg shape from the opposite diagonal. Attach a band around the third peg up in the second column, and connect it to the next peg to the right and down. Move up to the next diagonal row, starting on the fourth peg up all the way on the left, and lay out a diagonal row of bands moving to the right and down. Repeat until you have filled in the whole egg shape this way.

6. Triple-loop a cap band around the bottom peg on the loom.

7. Start at the peg that you triple-looped a cap band and hook the band just below the cap band. Pull the band up and off the peg, and loop it back onto the peg where it started. Do the same with the other bands on the peg, working your way down. Move to the next peg and do the same. Loop all of

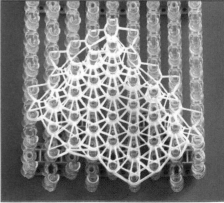

the pegs in the egg shape this way, moving from one end of the shape to the other.

8. Secure the final loose loops with a c-clip and remove the shape from the loom.

9. Repeat steps 1 to 9 to make more eggs.

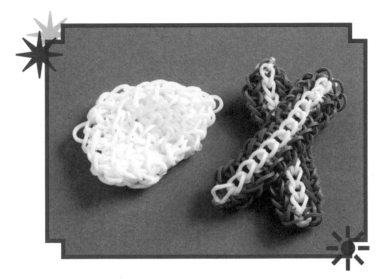

PONYTAIL HOLDER

Get a trio of fun with this zigzag ponytail holder! Hair elastics can be boring, so this stylish rubber band project will add some pizzazz to any hairdo. Just attach these three colorful pendants to any hair elastic and have a sensational new hair accessory!

Difficulty level: **Easy**

You need:

1 loom • hook • 12 beads • 1 hair elastic • 38 rubber bands

1. Set up your loom with the middle column of the loom moved one peg closer to you and with the arrow facing away.

2. Starting at the first middle peg, lay out a zigzag pattern throughout the whole loom, switching back and forth between two of your colors, as shown.

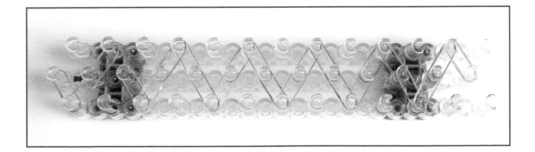

3. Using your other color bands, lay out a single chain of bands down the center column of your loom. On the second, sixth, and eleventh bands in the column, thread the band through a bead before placing the band on the loom as usual.

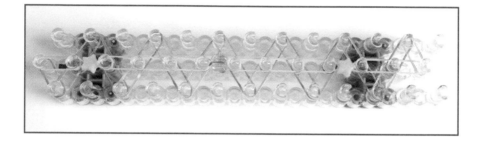

4. Triple-loop a cap band on the last peg of the middle column.

5. Starting from the cap band, loop the rubber bands from the center column only, looping each band back onto the peg where it started. Do this for the whole column.

6. Return to the cap band and loop the rubber bands from the zigzag pattern the same way you looped the center column. Make sure to follow the zigzag pattern as you loop.

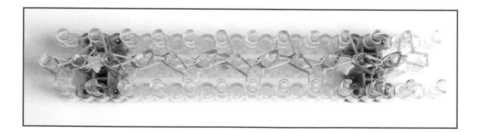

7. Using the same color rubber band as your center column, thread the band through a bead and tie a knot. Knot the beaded

rubber band around the bands on the last peg in the center column.

8. Remove the project from the loom—you may need to twist the last bead a little to make it appear right-side up.

9. Repeat these steps two more times to create the other dangly pendants. Try switching the placement of your colors for a different look!

10. Using the non-beaded end of one of the pendants, grab hold of the first rubber band and knot it around your hair elastic. You will wrap the rubber band around the hair elastic and pull the pendant through the loop of the band. Pull tight to secure. Do this for each of the pendants, and you are ready to go!

SWEETHEART NECKLACE

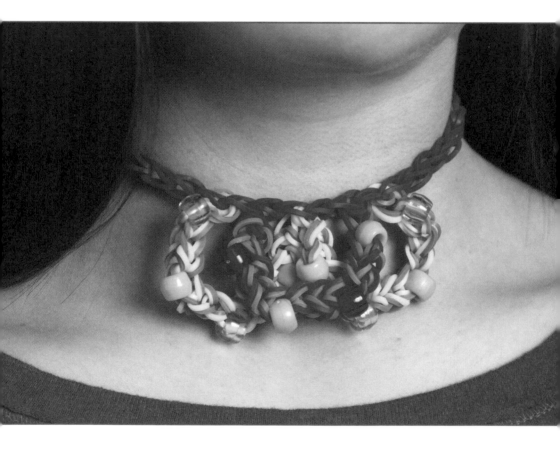

Make this necklace for someone special, for a special occasion, or just as a gift to yourself! The dangly loops on this necklace make a typical rubber band necklace into something extravagant. Try this with any of your favorite colors and beads to add something fun and unique to your collection of rubber band jewelry!

Difficulty level: **Easy**

You need:

1 loom • hook • c-clip • 12 beads • about 72 rubber bands

1. Set up the loom with a single column and the arrow pointing away from you.

2. Attach two bands to the first peg and connect them to the next peg. Thread a pair of bands through a pony bead, and attach them to the second and third pegs.

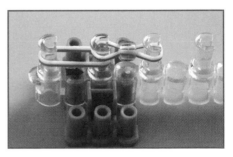

3. Continue laying out bands in this way, laying out two bands at a time and threading a bead

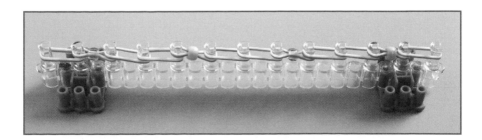

through every third pair of bands, until you reach the end of the loom.

4. Start at the second to last peg in the column, and loop your bands back to the peg where they started.

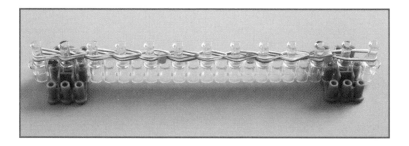

5. Once you've looped all the bands in this way, thread a single band through the loose bands left on the peg closest to you. Secure the single band with a c-clip, and remove the project from the loom.

6. Repeat steps 1 through 4 two more times to make three total chains. Make two chains in the same two colors (pink and white in our example) and the third chain slightly different (pink and red in our example). Set all three chains aside.

7. Set up your loom with a single column and the arrow pointing away from you. Lay out a line of single bands, starting at the peg closest to you and working your way to the end of the loom.

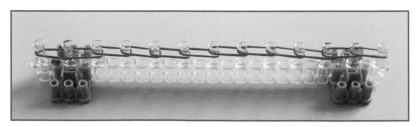

8. Turn your loom so the arrow is pointing toward you. Start at the second peg in the column, and loop your bands back to the peg where they started.

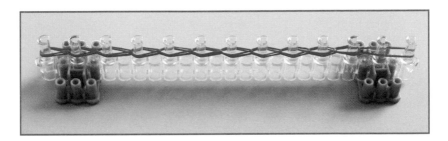

9. Secure the loose loops on the final peg with a c-clip or with your plastic hook. Pull the chain off the loom and set it aside.

10. Lay out a single chain of bands down the loom as you did in step 7. Once you have laid out your bands, take the single chain you set aside in step 9, and slide the loose loops onto the last peg in the column on top of the last band you placed.

11. Arrange the patterned chains on the loom on top of the chain you just laid out. Find the center peg in the column (the seventh peg from the end), and stack the c-clipped ends of the matching chains onto this peg. Remove the c-clips. Double-loop the other end of each chain to the third peg from the center, each in opposite directions.

12. Place the third chain onto the middle of the loom on top of the other chains: put the c-clipped end onto the peg to the left of the center peg, and double-loop the other end to the peg to the right of the center peg.

13. Turn your loom so the arrow points toward you. Start at the second peg in the column and loop your bands back to the peg where they started.

14. Secure the loops on the final peg with a c-clip or your plastic hook and carefully remove the bands from the loom.

15. Lay out a single chain of bands all the way down the loom. Stack the loops from step 14 on top of the last band you laid out. Starting at this peg, loop your bands back to the peg where they started.

16. Secure the last loops with a c-clip. Remove your project from the loom.

FASHiON JeWeLRY STAND

This project uses the fish stitch to make the strands on the jewelry stand. The directions below explain how to make the stitch on a loom. For instructions on a mini-loom, refer to the Octopus or Covered Hoop Earrings instructions, and then return to this page for the rest of the project.

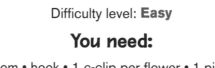

Difficulty level: **Easy**

You need:

1 loom • hook • 1 c-clip per flower • 1 picture frame • 8 tacks • glue or tape • 26 rubber bands per strand (colors shown for one strand: 10 green, 8 pink, 8 red) • 19 rubber bands per flower (colors shown: 6 pink, 6 red, 7 yellow)

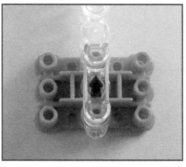

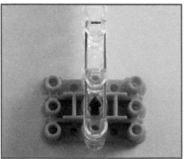

For the Strands Using a Loom:

1. Each strand for the jewelry stand requires one column from a loom. Set up this column with the arrow facing away from you.

2. Attach a green band to the first peg, and connect it to the second peg.

3. Attach a red band to the first peg, and connect it to the third peg.

4.   Repeat this process for each peg up the loom, switching between your colors: instead of connecting two pegs with each band, you will be connecting three.

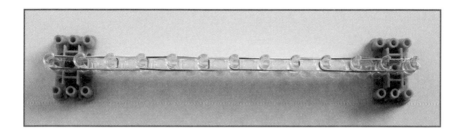

5.   Attach a green band to the second to last peg on the loom, and connect it to the last peg.

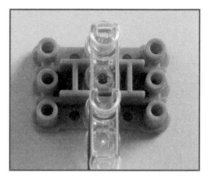

6.   From the second to last peg, take your hook and loop each band back to the peg where it started. Do this for the whole loom.

7.   This is the first half of one strand. Securing it with a temporary

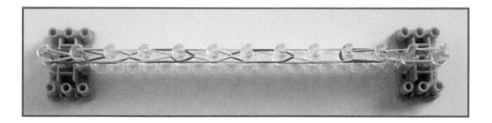

c-clip, remove this strand from the loom and set it aside to attach to the other half later.

8.   Repeat steps 2 through 4 for the second half of the strand.

9. Take the loose band from your first strand, and stretch the end of it onto the last two pegs on the loom, as you did with the last band in step 5.

10. Begin looping this set of rubber bands back to the pegs where they started. Do this for the whole loom.

11. Attach a temporary c-clip, pull the project off the peg, and set it aside. Repeat steps 1 through 7 for each additional strand for about four to six strands.

For the Flower:

1. Using a full loom, set the middle column one peg closer to you with the arrow pointing away.

2. Beginning on the second middle peg, lay out a hexagon on your pegs with red rubber bands: start on the middle peg and create the left half of a hexagon, moving clockwise. Return to the middle peg, and place bands down for the right half of the hexagon, going counterclockwise.

3. With your yellow bands, lay out the inner "petals," starting from the top right peg within the hexagon and moving clockwise around, as shown.

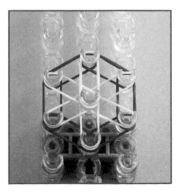

4. Using your pink rubber bands, lay out six outer "petals." The petals should go from pegs one to two for all three columns and from pegs three to four for all three columns.

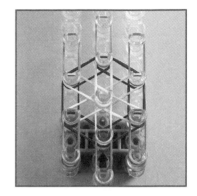

5. Double-loop a yellow cap band in the center peg of your flower.

6. Starting with the yellow "petals," loop the bands with your hook back to the peg where they started in the order in which you placed them on the loom. Start with the band that is closest to the top, below the cap band.

7. Loop each red band back to the peg where it started, working in reverse order of how you placed them on the loom (begin with the top middle and move to the right down to the bottom middle peg, then loop from the top middle peg and move left down to the bottom middle peg). You do not loop the pink outer "petals."

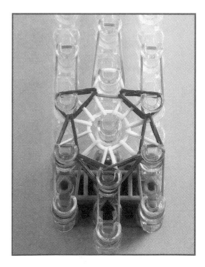

8. Attach a c-clip to the bottom, and remove the flower from the loom.

9. Repeat these steps for more flowers.

Assembling the Jewelry Stand:

1. Insert eight tacks into the back of a picture frame, spreading them evenly apart, as shown.

2. To attach the strands to the frame, wrap a band from one end of a long strand around a tack. (Any c-clips should be removed.) Wrap the strand across the front of the frame, and wrap the band from the opposite end of the strand around the tack directly across from the first one.

3. Repeat this for each set of strands.

4. Use glue or tape to attach your flowers, placing them along the frame any way you like.

5. Hang jewelry from the strands. For studded earrings, just make sure to insert the pierced parts through the strand and secure them with the earring backs so they don't fall off the strand.

GLOW-iN-THE-DARK STARS

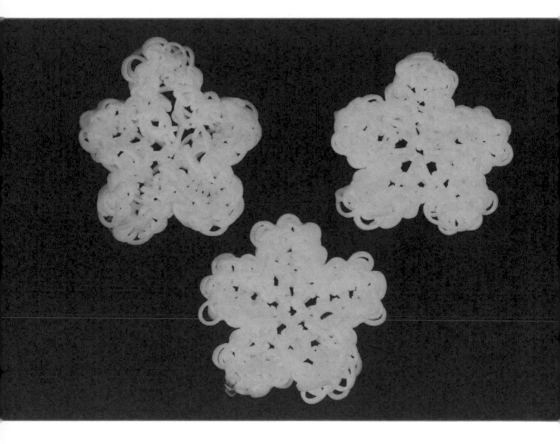

Light up your room with these handmade constellations! Hang them from the ceiling with some string, or make a vast night sky in your bedroom by fixing them with sticky tack. Learn about constellations like Orion or the Big Dipper and form them in your own room! This project requires three looms, so team up with some friends and put your looms together to make these shining stars! Anything that glows in the dark usually needs to soak up some light first, so just make sure to keep the project in lots of light before you want it to glow in the dark.

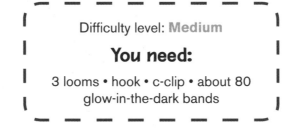

Difficulty level: **Medium**

You need:

3 looms • hook • c-clip • about 80
glow-in-the-dark bands

1. Set up three looms side by side with the pegs square and the arrows pointing toward you.
2. Begin laying your star shape out onto the loom: attach a band to the first middle peg on the loom, and connect it up and to the left.
3. Lay out a horizontal line of two bands going up from the peg where you ended your last band.
4. Lay out a line of two bands, moving to the left.
5. Attach a band to the peg where you ended your last horizontal band, and connect to the next peg up and to the left. Attach another band to this peg, and connect it up and to the right.
6. Lay out a line of two bands going to the right.
7. Lay out two diagonal bands going up and to the left. Attach a band to the last peg you connected, and connect it two pegs above it and to the left, on the far left edge.
8. Attach a band to the last peg, and connect it to the next peg two to the right and one down.

9. Lay out a line of two diagonal bands going down and to the right, ending in the middle above the middle peg where you started.

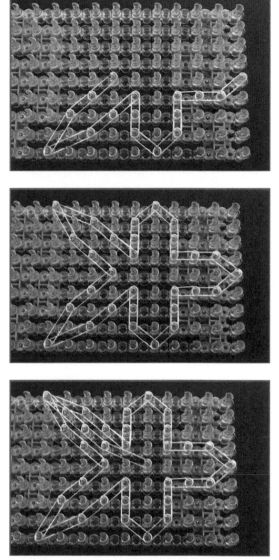

10. Start at the first middle peg, and lay out the right side of the star shape just as you did the left side, laying out your bands in the opposite direction.

11. Begin filling in your star shape with bands: start at the top right point, and lay out a diagonal line of four bands, ending on the middle peg in the shape.

12. Start at the top left point, and lay out a diagonal line of four bands, ending on the middle peg of the shape.

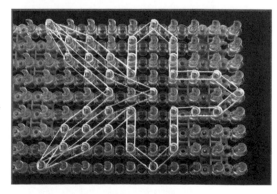

13. Lay out a line of bands from each remaining point of the star to the middle peg of the star shape. The lines should all start at the point and end in the center.

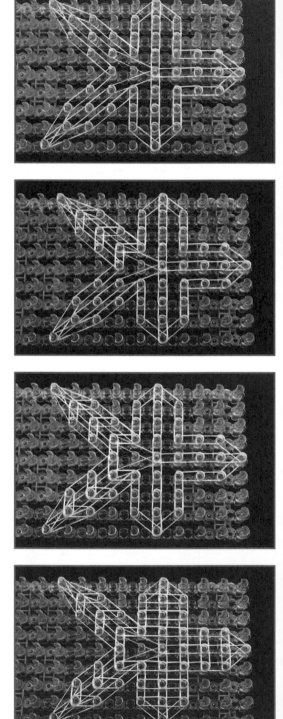

14. Lay out three arrow shapes along the top right point of your star: connect two bands to each center peg in the point and attach them to the pegs on either side.

15. Do the same for the top left point of your star shape.

16. Do the same for the rest of the points in your star shape: connect the pegs from the line of bands you laid down the center to the pegs on either side.

17. Double-loop a cap band around the center peg in the shape.

18. Start at the center peg where you just put the cap band and begin looping the bands inside your star shape back to the pegs where they started. Loop all the bands on the peg in this way before moving to the next peg. Make your way from the center peg to the end of each point in your star shape. Do not loop the outer bands.

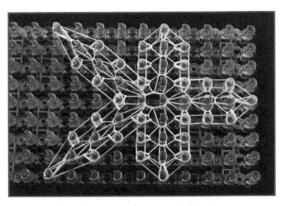

19. Loop the outer bands of your star shape: start on the seventh middle peg, and loop first the right side and then the left side of your star shape, moving in the opposite direction from how you laid the bands onto the loom.

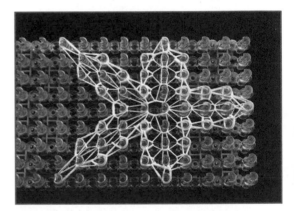

20. Secure the loose loops from the final peg with a c-clip. Carefully remove your star from the loom.

LOOPY BRACELET

This bracelet is a cinch to make and is great for both boys and girls. The loopy stitch can be worn on its own, but if you would like to get a little fancy, try adding the decorative flower or even a sports bead! (Instructions for a flower decoration are located on the same page as the Fashion Jewelry Stand.) You can make this project in all sorts of colors and even make matching friendship bracelets!

Difficulty level: **Easy**

You need:

1 loom • hook • 2 c-clips
For the bracelet: 12 white bands • 18 gold bands • 18 purple bands
For the flower: 6 white bands, 7 orange bands, 6 purple bands

1. Set up the loom with the middle column moved one peg closer to you and with the arrow facing away.

2. Lay out a line of single bands along the middle column of the loom.

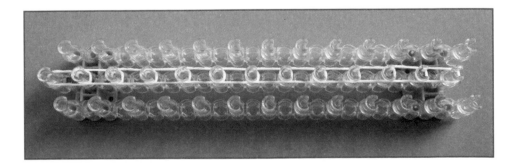

3. Starting with the first peg, make a triangle with your rubber bands. Attach one rubber band to the first middle peg, and connect it to the first left peg. Attach another rubber band to the first middle peg, and connect it to the first right peg. Attach a rubber band to the first left peg, and connect it to the first right peg to finish your triangle.

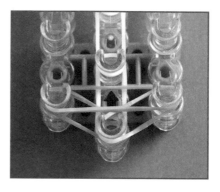

4. Repeat this step to create a total of twelve triangles across the whole loom. Alternate your colors for each triangle shape.

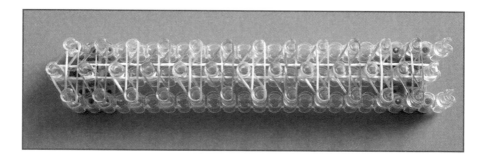

5. Turn your loom so that the arrow is pointing toward you. Starting at the middle peg closest to you, loop only the white bands back to the pegs where they started. Do this for the whole loom.

6. Loop the two diagonal parts of the purple and orange triangles to the pegs where they started. Start from the triangle closest to you (the last triangle that you put down) and continue to the end of the loom. Do not loop any of the horizontal bands in the triangles.

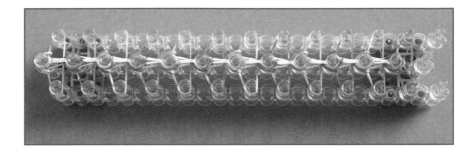

7. Attach a c-clip to the end of the project and remove carefully from the loom.

8. To create a flower attachment, see the Fashion Jewelry Stand. The flowers there are the same as in this project, just switch up your colors!

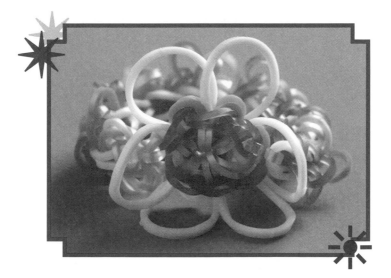

ZIPPER DECORATION

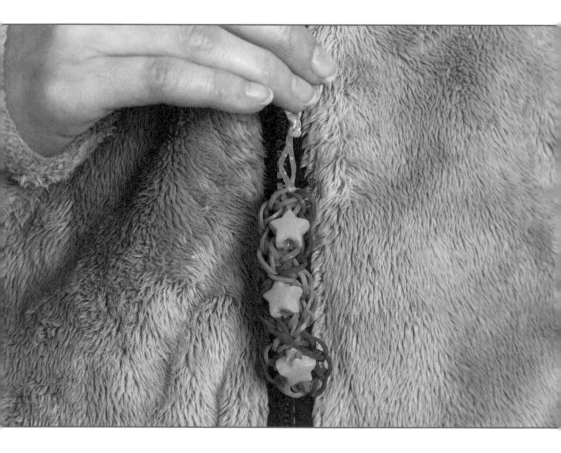

Put the *zip* back in your zipper with this cool creation! This project is so quick and easy, you'll want to make one for every zipper you own. With a quick color and bead change, you can make this decoration match any ensemble.

Difficulty level: **Easy**

You need:

1 loom • hook • 3 beads • a craft or zipper clip • 34 bands

1. Set up your loom with the middle pegs set one peg closer to you and the arrow pointing away from you.

2. Starting at the first middle peg, lay out the right side of a hexagon shape: connect one band up and to the right, then lay out a line of two bands up the right column, then connect a band up and to the left to the fourth center peg.

3. Lay out the left side of the hexagon in the same way, ending on the fourth middle peg.

4. Lay out two more hexagon shapes in the same way, alternating the colors as shown.

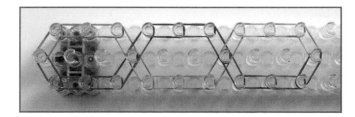

5. Lay out a line of bands down the center of your loom, starting at the first middle

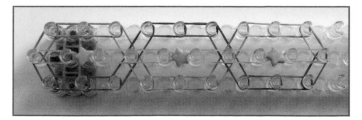

peg and ending where you ended your third hexagon shape. Thread a bead around the middle band of each hexagon before putting the band on the loom.

6. Double-loop a cap band over the last peg in your pattern.

7. Start at your double-looped peg, and loop your bands back to the peg where they started. Continue looping your project until all of the bands have been looped back to their starting peg, making your way back to the start of the loom.

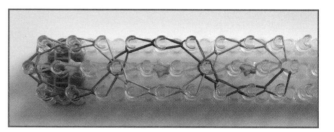

8. Loop a band through the loose loops on the first middle peg, and tie it off to secure them.

9. Remove the project from the loom. Use the band from the last step to attach your project to a zipper clip.

WRISTLET

Carry your stuff right on your wrist: this little pouch can hold some lunch money, a lucky penny, or maybe a note from someone special! Just put the bead through some bands in the flap to close the pouch and keep your stuff safe.

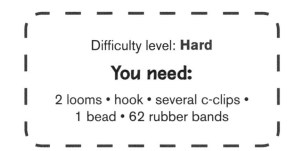

Difficulty level: **Hard**

You need:

2 looms • hook • several c-clips •
1 bead • 62 rubber bands

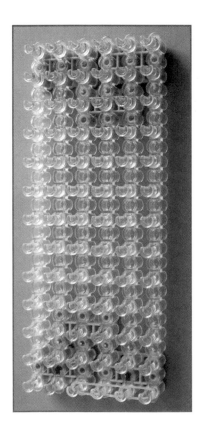

1. Set up two looms side by side with the arrows pointing away from you.

2. In the first row, lay out a line of three bands, starting at the far right corner and working right to left.

3. Attach a band to each of the four pegs you just connected, and connect them to the peg above. On the fourth peg, all the way on the left, connect a diagonal band to the next peg up and to the left.

4. Start on the far right peg in the second row, and lay out a row of four bands, moving from right to left.

5. Attach vertical bands to each of the pegs you connected in the second row, as you did in step 3. On the far left peg, connect a diagonal band to the next peg up and to the left.

6. Lay out a line of five bands across the pegs you just connected in the third row, moving from right to left.

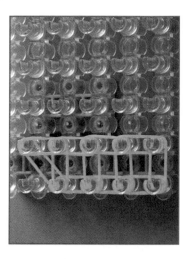

7. Starting on the right, connect each peg in the third row to the next peg above it. Connect the last peg on the left diagonally to the next peg up and to the right instead of directly above it.

8. Lay out a line of four bands across the fourth row going from right to left.

9. Starting on the right, connect each peg in the fourth row to the next peg above it. When you reach the second peg from the end, do not connect it to the peg above; connect it diagonally up and to the right.

10. Lay out a line of three bands across the fifth row, starting on the right and moving from right to left.

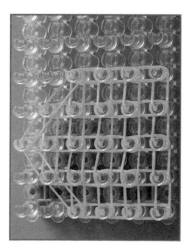

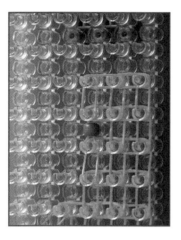

11.   Attach a band to each of the first three pegs from the right in the fifth row, and connect them to the peg above them. Move up to the next row and lay out a line of two bands, moving from the far right peg to the left. Repeat this pattern three more times to finish the front side of your pouch. For the last diagonal band between rows seven and eight, thread a bead onto the band before putting it on the loom: this button will let you fasten your wristlet pouch closed.

12. Double-loop a cap band over the peg where you looped your last band (the third peg from the right in the ninth row).

13. Turn your looms so the arrow is pointing toward you. Starting at the double-looped peg, loop your bands back to the pegs where they started. When you have finished looping the first peg, continue looping the row from right to left, then move to the next row. Loop the first four rows this way. For the next four rows, start by looping the middle peg (the third peg from the left, in the same column where you started looping each previous row). Loop from the center to the outside edges of the row before moving to the

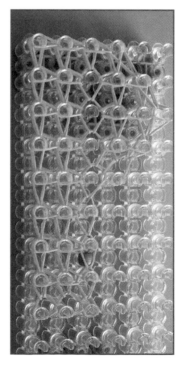

next row. On the final row on the loom, loop the peg on the far right first, then loop the rest of the row moving from right to left.

14. Secure the final loose loops with a c-clip. Remove the project from the loom.

15. Use a c-clip to attach the front part of the pouch to the back, then use another c-clip to close the bottom of the pouch.

16. Use several c-clips to attach your wristlet pouch to your favorite bracelet design.

GLOW-iN-THE-DARK ALiEN

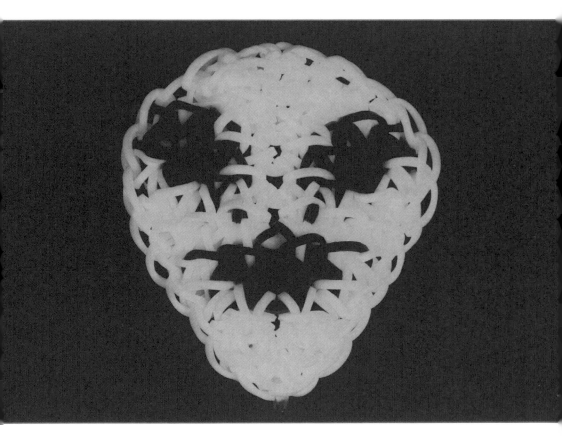

Try a rubber band project that is out of this world! This creepy alien is already a cool project, but watch what happens when the lights go out! His glowing head will be a great decoration for your room or for Halloween, and he goes well with the glow-in-the-dark stars from this book. Anything that glows in the dark usually needs to soak up some light first, so just make sure to keep the project in lots of light before you want it to glow in the dark.

Difficulty level: Medium

You need:

3 looms • hook • c-clip • 95 white glow-in-the-dark bands • 34 black bands

1. Set up three looms side by side with the pegs square and the arrows pointing away from you.

2. Begin laying the "alien" shape onto your loom: begin on the first middle peg, and loop the left half of the shape onto the loom in a clockwise direction, as shown. Then start again at the first middle peg and loop the right half, moving counter-clockwise.

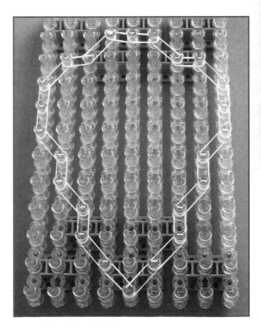

3. Start filling in your alien head shape. Attach a band to the first middle peg, and connect it to the next peg above.

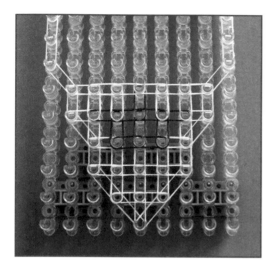

4. In the next row of your shape, lay out a horizontal line of bands, starting at the outside of the shape and moving toward the middle. Repeat this pattern all the way to the sixth row: lay out vertical bands from each peg inside the shape; then in the next row, lay out a horizontal line of bands across the alien head shape, starting at the outside edge and moving toward the middle of the row. Use black bands for the mouth, as shown.

5. Lay out vertical bands to connect the sixth row to the seventh row as you did for the other rows. Lay out your horizontal line across the seventh row as usual, using black bands for the eyes. When you lay out the vertical bands from the seventh to the

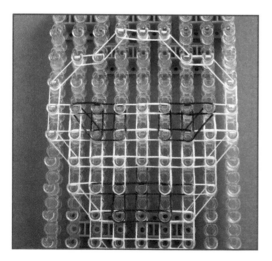

eighth row, place two additional black bands diagonally, from the third peg from the outside on either side to the next peg up and out. These bands are for the eyes.

6. Lay out your horizontal line across the eighth row, starting at the outside of the shape and moving toward the middle. Use black bands for the eyes, as shown.

7. Lay out your vertical bands from the eighth to the ninth row. Add four diagonal black bands for the eye shapes: connect the pegs on either side of the middle peg to the next peg up and

toward the outside. Connect the third pegs from the center to the next pegs up and out to continue the diagonal line from the last step.

8. In the next row (the ninth row), lay out a horizontal line of bands, starting at the outside of the shape and moving toward the middle. Use black bands for the eyes.

9. Lay out diagonal bands from the ninth row to the tenth, starting from the outside pegs and working your way to the middle.

10. Lay out a line of four bands across the tenth row, starting from the outside pegs and working your way to the middle.

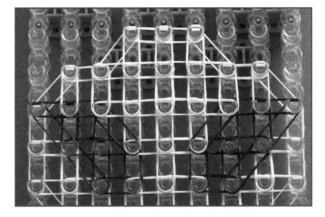

11. Lay out diagonal bands to connect the tenth row to the eleventh.

12. Double-loop a cap band over the middle peg in the top row of your shape.

13. Starting at the triple-looped peg, hook the first band beneath the triple-loop, and pull it up and off the peg, looping it back onto the peg where it started. Loop the middle peg in the row first, then loop the rest of the row,

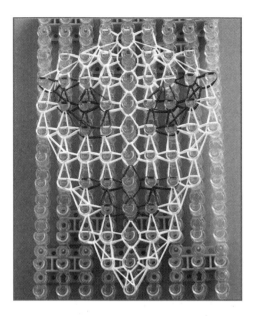

working your way from the middle toward the outside of the shape (in the opposite way that you laid out the bands). Then move down to the next row and loop it in the same way, working from the inside out.

14. Secure the bands on the final peg with a c-clip. Carefully remove your project from the loom.

15. To add alien nostrils, cut a rubber band with scissors and pull the band through the middle of the figure using your hook. Tie the band off in the back of the figure, and repeat for the other nostril.

HOCKEY STICK

Practice your puck handling with this cool mini hockey stick. Put together enough sticks and you can make a whole team. You can even change up the colors to match your favorite team's jersey! You can make poof ball pucks by following the instructions for the Poof Ball Bracelet and separating them or just one by not filling up the whole loom with poofs. This project requires cutting craft wire, which can be sharp, so please make sure to ask for permission or help from an adult beforehand.

Difficulty level: **Medium**

You need:

1 loom • hook • c-clip • about 6 inches of 18-gauge craft wire • small pliers or jewelry tools to cut and bend craft wire • 73 blue bands • 40 black bands

1. Set up one loom square with the arrow pointing away from you.

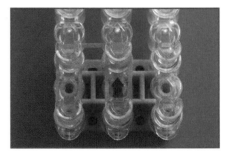

2. Connect a band from the first middle peg to the peg above it. Do the same for the first peg on the left. Connect a band from the middle peg in the second row to the peg to the left.

3. Repeat this pattern up the loom, laying out two vertical bands side by side then one band across the columns in the next row.

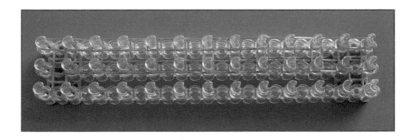

4. Triple-loop a cap band on the last middle peg on the loom.

5. Lay your craft wire over the loom between the two columns you laid out. Bend over the end of the wire so the sharp edge isn't sticking out.

6. Starting at the peg with the cap band, loop your bands back to the pegs where they started, looping over the craft wire as you go. Start with the middle peg and loop each peg in the row before moving down to the next row.

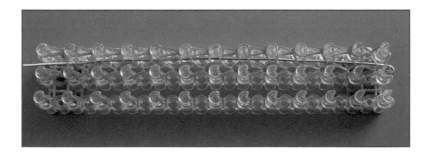

7. Use a c-clip or your plastic hook to secure the loose loops from the final two pegs for now. Carefully remove the bands from the loom and set aside.

8. Repeat steps 1 through 3, laying the two-column pattern onto the loom again. Take the wire and bands you set aside, and slide the loose loops onto the last two pegs on the loom as shown, with the wire running between the columns like last time.

9. Loop your bands over the craft wire as before, starting with the middle peg in the last row and working your way to the other end of the loom. Secure the final loops with a c-clip or your plastic hook and set it aside.

10. Set up your loom square again with the arrow pointing away from you.

11. Starting at the bottom left peg, lay out a line of two bands across the row, moving from left to right.

12. Lay out vertical bands connecting each peg in the first row to the peg above it.

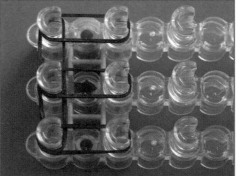

13. Repeat step 12 up the rest of the loom, ending with the horizontal line across the ninth row.

14. Take the project you have set aside and slide it onto the last two pegs in the far left column. Bend the wire so it lies

between the middle and left columns.

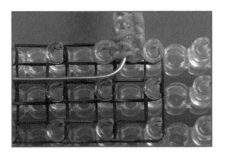

15. Starting with your far left peg in the ninth row, begin looping your bands back to the pegs where they started. When you loop bands between the middle and left columns, loop your bands over the wire. Move from left to right in each row before moving down to the next row until you have looped all the bands on the loom.

16. Secure the loose bands from the last peg with a c-clip. Carefully remove the bands from the loom. Trim the wire and tuck in the sharp edges.

WRAP BRACELET

This wrap bracelet is rainbow chic! By adding a bendable wire to a simple stitch, your rubber band bracelet becomes a one-of-a-kind fashion statement! Use a rainbow of colors like the one shown, or pick your own colors to make this unique to you! This project requires the cutting of craft wire, so make sure to ask an adult for permission or help before you begin. Like the photos shown, you can complete this project using one loom; if you have two looms at home, put them together to make one long loom so that you can complete the project with fewer steps.

Difficulty level: **Easy**

You need:

1 loom • hook • 1 bendable craft wire the length of two looms (about 24 inches) • pair of pliers or wire cutters • 50 rubber bands of varying colors

1. Set up your loom so that the middle column is one peg closer to you and the arrow is pointing away.

2. Using the center and left-hand columns, lay out a zigzag pattern with alternating colors: attach a rubber band to the first peg in the center column, and connect it to the first peg in the left column. Attach a band of the same color from that peg to the second peg in the center column, forming a V. Continue in

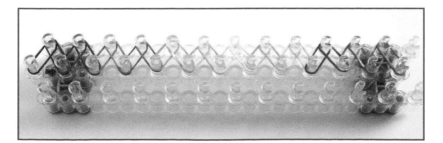

this way for the whole loom, making a zigzag that looks like a rainbow, starting with shades of red, then orange, then yellow, then green, then blue, and ending with purple.

3. Double-loop a cap band on the last peg of the loom.

4. Lay down your craft wire over the bands between the center and left-hand columns. Make sure the top of the craft wire is bent so that the bands will not come off and so that you will not pinch yourself. If the wire is very firm, use pliers to bend the ends. Do not cut the wire—it is longer than the loom on purpose.

5. Starting from the peg with the cap band and working backward, loop the bands back to the pegs where they started. Be careful to keep the wire in place as you loop back the bands.

6. Attach a c-clip to the end of the project, remove it from the loom, and set it aside.

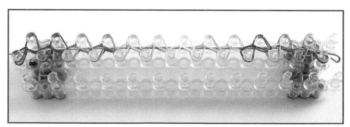

7. Repeat steps 1 and 2; this will be the other half of your wrap bracelet.

8. Take the first half of the wrap bracelet that has the wire already in it and remove the c-clip, being careful not to let the bracelet

unravel. Attach the end where the wire is sticking out around the very last center peg on the loom. The wire should be over the new rubber bands and between the center and left-hand columns.

9. You will not need a cap band, since the loop in the first half of the bracelet will act like one. Starting from here where the bracelets connect, loop the bands back to the pegs where they started until you reach the other end of the loom.

10. Attach a c-clip to secure the last loose loops

11. Bend the wire inward so that the bands do not slide off and so that there are no sharp edges.

12. Using your arm as a guide, bend the project to be bracelet-shaped. If you would like the bracelet to look like the one in the photo, form wide circles and stretch the bracelet outward. If you would like the bracelet to be more like a cuff, form tighter circles that are closer together.

BLOODSHOT EYEBALLS

This eyeball project is creepy and has extra ick-factor! Whether you use them to gross out all your friends or to wear them over your own eyes, these baby blues are double the fun! Try them out with your own eye color or even invent a new one, like orange or rainbow. While these eyes probably won't do much good for your vision, they will be an awesome addition to your rubber band project collection!

> Difficulty level: **Medium**
>
> ## You need:
>
> 3 looms • hook • 2 c-clips • about 89 white glow-in-the-dark bands • 11 red bands • 16 blue bands (or other eye color) • 4 black bands

1. Set up three looms side by side with the pegs square and the arrow pointing away from you.

2. Lay out a trapezoid shape on your loom to start the eyeball. Attach a white band to the center peg in the first row, and connect it to the peg to the right. Attach another band to each of these pegs, and connect them to the next peg up and away from the center. Attach another band to each, and connect it to the next peg above. Lay out a line of three horizontal bands across the second row, starting on the peg on the left where you ended your diagonal band and moving from left to right.

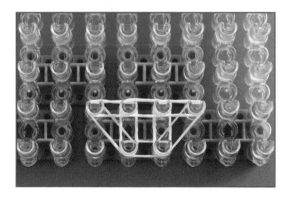

3. Continue to expand your eyeball shape in the same way you laid out your trapezoid. Attach bands to the outside pegs in the line you laid out in the second row, and connect them to the next pegs up and away from the center. Lay out diagonal bands to connect the four pegs in the second row to the next pegs above. To add the red bloodshot bands, attach additional diagonal bands on top of your white vertical bands before laying your horizontal line across the next row. You can either follow the example or lay your red bands at random.

4. When you reach the fourth row, use a blue band (or another eye color) for the middle horizontal band as you lay them out from left to right. When you lay out the vertical bands from the fourth to the fifth row, lay out the white bands on the three outside pegs on either side, then use blue bands for the center vertical bands. Attach an additional blue band to each of the center pegs, and connect them to the next peg up and away from the center.

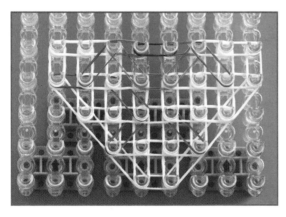

5. Lay out a horizontal line across the fifth row, moving from left to right. Use blue bands for the iris and a black band for the pupil, as shown. Add additional red bands next to the blue iris bands.

6. Finish laying out the iris and pupil of your eye, following the same pattern as before, laying out vertical bands then laying out a horizontal line across the row from left to right. When you lay out the vertical bands from row six to seven, lay out the white bands on the three outside pegs on either side, then lay out the blue diagonal bands moving up and toward the middle. Lay the two vertical blue

bands last. Lay out your horizontal line across the seventh row, changing colors when necessary. Add additional red bands near the iris.

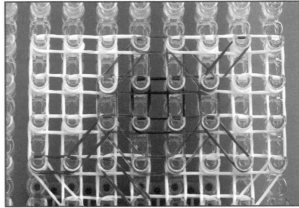

7. Continue laying out your eye shape, laying out diagonal bands then a line of horizontal bands. Use diagonal bands on the outside pegs of the shape to make the rows shorter as you move toward the top of the loom in the same way you increased them in the first half of the project until you reach the tenth row.

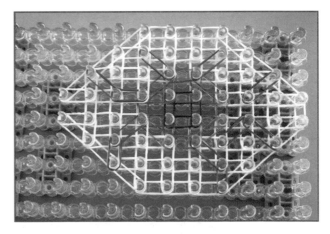

8. Double-loop a cap band around the two middle pegs in the tenth row.

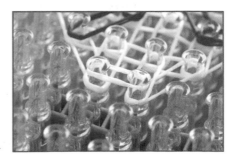

9. Loop the bands in your project back to the pegs where they started, starting with the bands on the pegs where you placed your cap band. Move from left to right then move down to the next row until you reach the end of the loom.

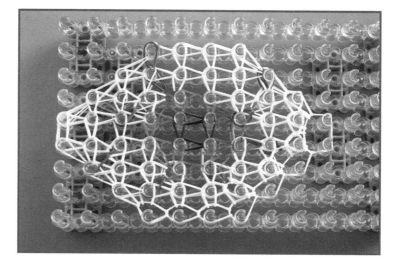

10. Secure the loose loops remaining on the loom with a c-clip, and remove your eyeball from the loom.

11. Repeat these steps to make more eyeballs.

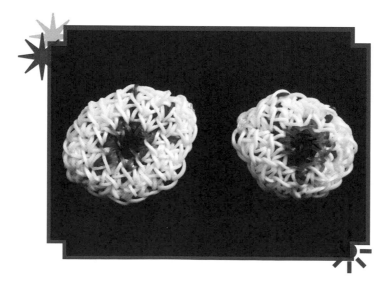

GLOW-iN-THE-DARK GHOST

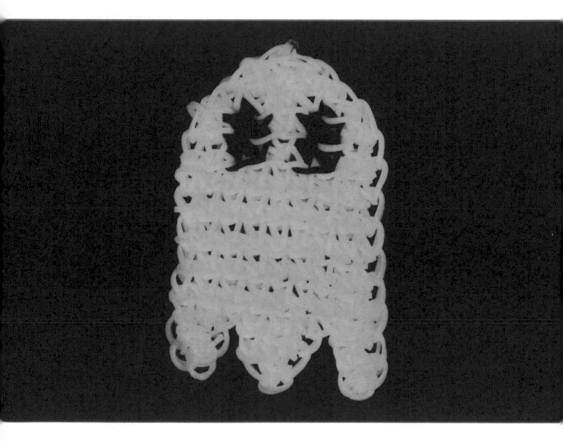

Make your loom skills glow with this awesome phantom of the dark! This ghoul is pretty simple to make and can be used for all sorts of things when you are done. Tie him to a string and hang him from the ceiling so he looks like he is suspended in midair at night, or glue him to a magnet and stick him on the fridge so you can see him glow when you grab a midnight snack! Anything that glows in the dark usually needs to soak up some light first, so just make sure to keep the project in lots of light before you want it to glow in the dark.

Difficulty level: **Easy**

You need:

3 looms • hook • c-clip, 171 white glow-in-the-dark bands • 8 black bands

1. Set up three looms side by side with the pegs square and the arrow pointing away from you.

2. You will start the figure by laying out a trapezoid, using the white bands. Lay out a horizontal line of two bands across the first row of the middle loom, moving from left to right. Then attach a band to each of the outside pegs of the middle loom, and connect them to the next peg up and away from the center. Lay out a horizontal line of four bands across the second row, starting where you ended your diagonal band on the left and moving from left to right to complete the trapezoid shape.

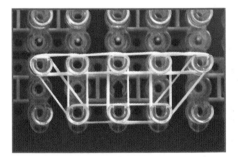

3. From here, you will make the trapezoid larger. Attach a band to the pegs on the outside edges of your trapezoid in the second

row, and connect them diagonally to the next peg up and away from the center.

4. Attach a band to each peg in the second row of your shape, and connect them to the pegs directly above in the third row.

5. Lay out a horizontal line of six bands across the third row, starting on the peg on the left where you attached your diagonal band, and moving from left to right. Use black for the second and fifth bands for the eyes.

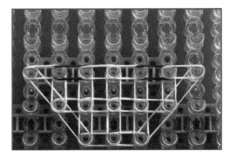

6. Make your trapezoid shape larger one more time. Starting with the left corner peg of your trapezoid, attach a band diagonally to the next row up and to the left. Repeat this on the right side, going right.

7. Starting from the third row on the trapezoid, connect a band vertically to the peg directly above it. Use black rubber bands for the eyes, on the second, third, fifth, and sixth pegs of the trapezoid.

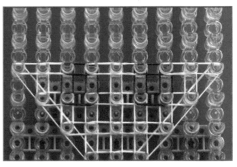

8. For the next row, lay down nine vertical bands, all using the glow-in-the-dark bands.

9. From these pegs, lay out eight horizontal bands from one peg to another, going from left to right.

10. Repeat steps 8 and 9 until you reach the tenth row on the loom.

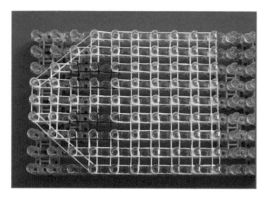

11. To make the bottom of the ghost, attach vertical bands to the pegs in the tenth row, and connect them to the eleventh row: attach bands to the three middle pegs and the two outside pegs on either side. Do not attach vertical bands to the third peg from the center on either side.

12. From the two pegs you skipped, attach bands diagonally to the next peg up and to the left and up and to the right in the eleventh row.

13. Lay out horizontal bands across the eleventh row, moving from left to right and skipping the third peg from the center on either side.

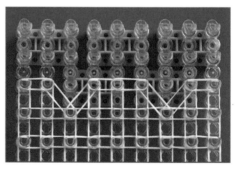

14. Attach vertical bands to the three middle pegs and the two outside pegs on either side in the eleventh row, and connect them to the pegs above in the twelfth row. Do not attach vertical bands to the third peg from the center on either side.

15. Lay out horizontal bands across the twelfth row, moving from left to right and skipping the third peg from the center on either side.

16. Attach a vertical band from the outside pegs in the twelfth row, and connect them to the next peg above, at the top corners of your loom. Attach a band to each of the top corner pegs, and

connect it to the next peg
down and toward the center
to make a triangle. Attach a
band to the middle peg in
the twelfth row, and connect
it to the peg above. Attach a
band to each peg on either

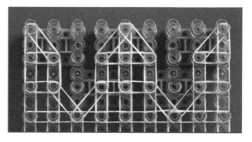

side of the middle peg in the twelfth row,
and connect them to the top middle peg
to make a triangle shape.

17. Attach a cap band to the tips of
    each triangle.

18. Turn the loom around so
    that the arrow is pointing
    toward you. Loop from
    each cap band to the
    fourth row from the end.
    Go from left to right for
    each part.

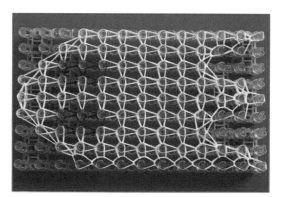

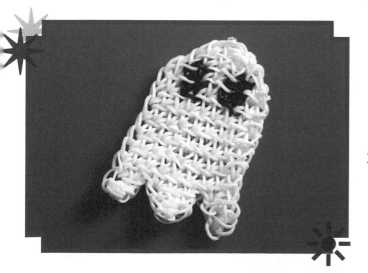

19. For the rest of the
    ghost, loop all of
    the bands back to
    the pegs where they
    started, moving
    from left to right.

20. Remove the
    ghost from the
    loom, and
    attach a c-clip.

BLACK BAT

Meet the rubber band Dracula! This awesome black bat is just like the real thing, with creepy yellow eyes and flapping wings. This guy doesn't come all in one piece: you will need to make the wings and body separately and then attach everything together at the end. When you have finished, you can attach some string and dangle him from your ceiling, or use him as a spooky accessory!

Difficulty level: **Hard**

You need:

2 looms • hook • 6–8 c-clips • about 340 black rubber bands • 2 yellow rubber bands

For the Body:

1. Set up two looms side by side with the pegs square and the arrows pointing away from you.

2. To start the base of the bat's body, you will be making a trapezoid. Place a band horizontally in the center two columns (the ones that connect the two looms). From the left center peg, attach a band up and to the left. From the right center peg, attach a band up and to the right. Connect these two bands by placing three horizontal bands across the second row of pegs.

3. Attach vertical bands to connect each of the four pegs in the second row of your shape to the pegs in the row above. Attach a band to the far left peg, and connect it to the next peg up and to the left. Then attach another band to the far left peg, and connect it to the peg above. Continue laying out vertical bands,

moving from left to right. Attach a second band to the far right peg and connect it up and to the right.

4. In the third row, lay horizontal bands moving from left to right across the row to form the trapezoid.

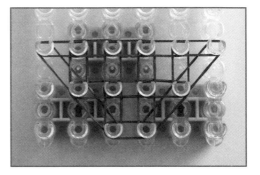

5. Continue your pattern for the next four rows: connect vertical bands from one row to the next, then lay out a horizontal line across the row, going from left to right. Repeat until you've reached the seventh row.

6. On the far left peg in the seventh row, attach a rubber band, and connect it diagonally to the next peg up and toward the middle of the loom. Lay out vertical bands from the next four pegs in the row, moving from left to right, then connect the last peg up and toward the middle. Move to the next row, and lay out a line of bands across the pegs you just connected. Repeat for the next row.

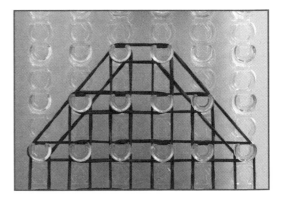

7. Lay out a circle shape above your trapezoid: this will be the bat's head. On the left middle peg of the ninth row (where you left off with the bat's body), attach a band and connect it up and to the left. Attach another band, and connect it to the peg above. Move to the right middle peg in the ninth row and attach a band. Connect it to the next peg above. Attach another band, and connect it up and to the right.

8. Lay out a line of three horizontal bands across these pegs, going from left to right. Attach a band to each of the four pegs in your last horizontal line, and connect them to the pegs directly above them. Then attach three horizontal bands across these pegs. From here, lay down a diagonal band from the far left peg in the figure to the peg up and to the right. Attach a peg from the left center peg to the one directly above it. Attach a band from the right center peg to the one directly above that one. On the far right peg in the figure, attach a band to the peg diagonally up and to the left. Connect the center two pegs with one horizontal band.

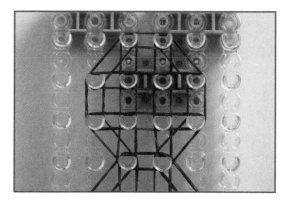

9. On either side of the bat's head shape, attach a band from the third to last row to the second to last row, parallel to where the head ends. Going from left to right, attach a band from the far

left peg of the figure to the center left peg, then connect a band from the center right peg to the far right peg. For the ears, you need to create two right-angle triangles. Attach a band from the far left

second to last peg to the peg directly above it. Attach a band from the center left peg diagonally to the peg up and to the left, completing the left ear. For the right ear, attach a band from the right center peg diagonally to the peg up and to the right. On the far right peg, attach a band to the one directly above it, completing the right ear.

10. Double-loop a cap band for each of the points of the ears, on the last two pegs in the loom.

11. Turn your loom around so that the arrow is pointing toward you. Using your hook, begin looping the bands back to the pegs where they started, going in reverse order of how you laid them down. Start with the right ear that is now on your left, and loop the band back to its original peg from under the cap band. Do this for

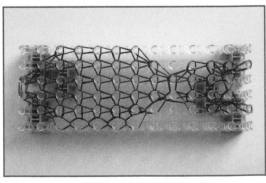

both ears, and then loop the rest of the bat shape, moving from left to right.

12. Attach a c-clip to the bottom of the bat's body and carefully remove from the loom.

13. Using two yellow rubber bands, weave eyes into the head of the bat using your hook. You can secure them using c-clips or by knotting them in the back of the bat's head.

For the Wings:

1. With your same two looms set up side by side and the arrow facing away, lay out four horizontal rubber bands, going from the far left peg in the first row to the second to last peg in the first row. Going from left to right, lay out five vertical rubber bands from the pegs in the first row to the pegs directly above them in the second row. Repeat this until you reach the third row. On the third row, lay your bands as you did in the first two rows, then add a triangle shape. To do that, connect a diagonal band, a horizontal band, and another diagonal band to the peg in the far right column.

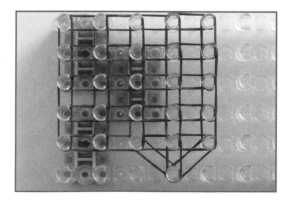

2. Repeat your wing pattern down the loom, stopping halfway through your third triangle on the tenth row.

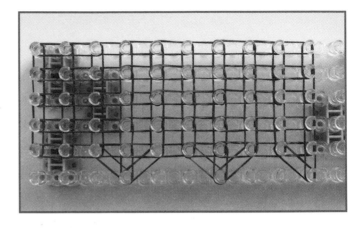

3. At the tenth row, attach a diagonal band from the far left column to the one up and to the right. Attach vertical bands to the next four pegs in the tenth row, and connect them to the row above them. On the last peg, attach a band diagonally up and to the left to finish the last triangle.

4. From the first column from the left, attach a band diagonally up and to the right. Attach two more vertical rubber bands in this row to the pegs directly above them.

5. In the second to last row, attach two horizontal bands.

6. From the outside peg in the second to last row, attach a band diagonally up and to the right, at the end of the loom. Attach vertical rubber bands for the remaining two columns.

7. Close off the wing by attaching a horizontal band across the two center pegs in the last row. Double-loop a cap band over one of the pegs in this row.

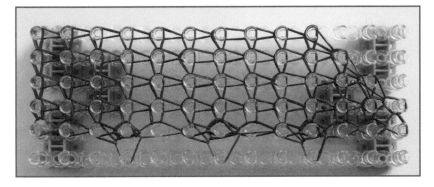

8. Turn the loom around so that the arrow is pointing toward you. Starting from the cap band, loop the bands back to the pegs where they started, going in reverse order of how you attached them on the loom.

9. Attach a c-clip and carefully remove from the loom.

10. Repeat these steps for the second wing.

11. To attach the wings to the body, thread two to three black bands through both sides of the body and then through the inside of each wing. Close these bands off with c-clips.

SERPENTINE BRACELET

This sssssuper stylish bracelet is made to look like a snake coiled around your wrist! As a slithering serpent that has red, black, and yellow coloring, this awesome bracelet is just like the infamous coral snake! Just give a snaky twist to a basic weave pattern for an awesome reptilian band!

Difficulty level: **Hard**

You need:

2 looms • hook • c-clip • 102 bands (colors shown: 38 yellow, 32 red, 32 black)

1. Set out two looms side by side with the columns square and the arrow pointing away from you.

2. Connect the two middle pegs in the first row with another yellow band.

3. Lay a line of yellow bands down each of the two middle columns of the loom. This will be the main strap of your bracelet.

4. Connect the two middle pegs in the second row with a yellow band.

5. Now you'll make the black and red loops that snake around this bracelet. Attach a black band to the first and second pegs in the right middle column, and connect them to the pegs to the right.

6. Lay out a black vertical band to connect the two pegs where you just ended your bands.

7. In the second column from the right, attach a band to the first and second pegs, then connect them to the next peg to the right.

8. Attach a band to the first and second peg in the far right column.

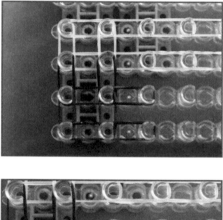

9. Repeat your square pattern as you lay out the red and black loops: attach black bands to the two pegs in the second row all the way to the right, and connect them to the next peg above. Connect the two pegs where you ended your bands with a yellow band.

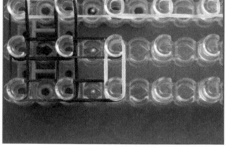

10. Lay out two vertical red bands from the pegs where you attached your last yellow band. Connect the pegs where you ended with a red horizontal band.

11. Lay out two vertical bands from the pegs where you attached your last red band. Connect the pegs where you ended with a red band.

12. In the fourth and fifth rows, attach a red band to the second peg from the right, and connect it to the next peg to the left, attaching your loop back to the main strap of the bracelet.

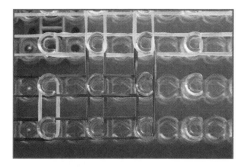

13. Connect the two middle pegs in the fourth and fifth row with yellow bands.

14. Continue laying out your snake loops as shown in the image, following the same pattern of laying out two parallel bands, then connecting them with a band going in the other direction. For each snake loop, you will lay out bands moving away from the center band, then moving toward the end of the loom, and finish the loop by working back to the center band. When you cross the center band, place yellow bands across the two middle pegs in the row, as you did in step 4 and step 13.

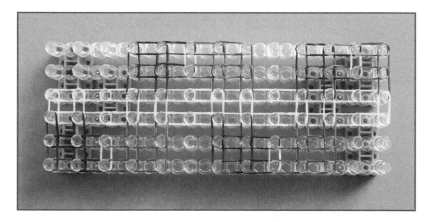

15. Triple-loop a cap band over the last peg in the pattern, the right middle peg at the end of the loom.

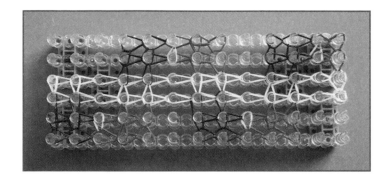

16. Turn the loom so the arrow is pointing toward you. Starting at the peg with the cap band, hook the first band beneath the triple-loop and pull it up and off the peg, looping it back onto the peg where it started. Always loop the top band on the peg first, then the next one down, until you have looped all of the bands on the peg. Continue looping the rest of the bands in this way, following the snake loops in the opposite direction that you laid them out.

17. Secure the last loose bands with a c-clip. If you want to make the bracelet longer, secure the last loose bands with a c-clip or your plastic hook and set it aside. Lay out the pattern on the loom again and stack the loose loops you set aside onto the last peg of the pattern, where you put your triple-looped cap band last time.

DiDDLY BOPPERS

Get excited about these fun loom head boppers! If you want to be a little festive or silly, or if you want to make a costume extra fun, this awesome headband is a great way to start! Many of the things you need for this project are materials you may have around your house, like a headband and pipe cleaners. Here we used a plastic headband, but cloth ones will work great, too! The project also requires two looms, so if you don't have an extra at home, team up with a friend and make them together!

Difficulty level: **Medium**

You need:

2 looms • hook • 2 c-clips • 2 lengths of 18-gauge craft wire (cut to 6–8 inches each) • 4 pipe cleaners • 42 beads • 1 headband • pliers or wire-cutters • 48 blue rubber bands • 12 pink rubber bands • 50 gold rubber bands • about 200 gold rubber bands for the headband (depending on how tightly packed you want the bands to be around the headband)

To Make the Boppers:

1. Set up two looms side by side with the pegs square and the arrow facing away from you.

2. Lay out a line of gold bands across the second row of the loom, starting on the far right peg and moving to the left.

3. Attach a pink band to a peg on the first row, and connect it vertically to the next peg in the second row. Do this for the whole first row.

4. Attach blue rubber bands vertically from the second pegs to the third pegs for the entire row. Thread a few of these bands through pony beads. (We chose to do every other, but doing them at random is fine, too!)

5. Repeat four more horizontal gold and three more vertical blue rows with pony beads as before. The last row of gold will not have beads.

6. From the last row where you put gold bands, attach a pink rubber band, and connect it vertically to to the next peg. Do this for the whole row.

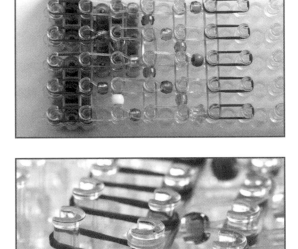

7. Double-loop a cap band over the second to last peg in the first row on the left.

8. Turn the loom around so that the arrow is pointing toward you.

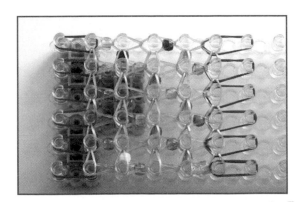

9. Loop the rubber bands back to the pegs where they started, going in reverse order of how you put them on the loom. Do not loop any of the pink bands.

10. Attach a c-clip to secure the project. Remove from the loom and set aside.

11. Repeat these steps for the second head bopper.

For the Headband:

1. Create a simple fish stitch chain with all your gold rubber bands. Using just the rubber bands and your fingers, loop one rubber through another and knot it on itself. This will hold the beginning of your stitch in place.

2. With the free rubber band, squish the band with your fingers so that it forms a half-moon shape.

3. Insert your next rubber band through the half moon.

4. Squish this band to form another half-moon. Insert another rubber band to repeat the process until you have a very long chain several times the length of the headband. If you are using a plastic headband, you may want to split this up into two chains on either side so that it is easier to slide the bands over the headband. This part can take some time.

5. Wrap each individual loop in the chain around the headband in order. For a neat, braided look like in the photograph, make sure that the part of the band that loops over the headband is the one that has the knot from the very next band. If you like a more zigzag look, then where you loop over the headband does not matter.

6. If your headband has a lot of teeth, it may take some effort to slide the rubber bands over the length of the headband; just go slowly.

7. Tie off the ends of the chain with a knot so that it does not come undone.

Connecting the Boppers with the Headband:

1. This part requires craft wire, which can sometimes poke or pinch. Please make sure to get permission from an adult when using the craft wire or have one help you. Cut two lengths of craft wire, about six to eight inches each.

2. Wrap one pipe cleaner around the length of each craft wire. Leave about two inches on either end exposed.

3. Slide one end of the craft wire through the diddly bopper. With about an inch or so of room, slide a bead over the top of the

wire. Bend the wire around the bead, and stick it back through the bopper. This bead will act as a cap so that the tip of the wire will not stick out. Do this for both boppers.

4. Wrap the other end of each wire around the headband, spreading them out evenly. If the wire is sticking out a lot, use pliers to press it closer to the stem of the bopper.

5. Wrap another pipe cleaner around the place where you wrapped the wire over the headband. This will make the wire feel soft and prevent it from poking you. Do this for both boppers.

6. You're ready to go!